BEGINNERS GUIDE To SELLING ON eBay 2024.

The art of a successful eBay selling.

By

RICHARD FRANKLIN.

Copyright © 2024 by (RICHARD FRANKLIN)

All rights reserved.

No part of this publication may be reproduced,distributed or transmitted in any form or by any means,including photocopying,recording,or other electronic or mechanical methods,without prior written permission of the publisher,expect in the case of brief quotations embodied in critical reviews and certain other noncommercial uses permitted by copyright law.

First Edition:July 2024

CONTENTS

INTRODUCTION... 5
The power of eBay ;Why sell here?
How this book will make you succeed

CHAPTER 1:.. 13
Creating Your eBay Seller Account... 13
    Setting Up Your Seller Profile.. 15
    Account Verification and Security on eBay................................. 18
    Understanding eBay's Selling Policies and Fees........................ 22
    Choosing Between Personal and Business Accounts.............. 24

Chapter 2:... 27
Researching and Selecting Products... 27
    Finding Your Niche: What Sells Best on eBay............................ 29
    Analyzing Market Trends and Demands..................................... 31
        Analysis of the Graph.. 33
    Sourcing Products:wholesales, Dropshipping and More......... 35

Chapter 3:... 37
Crafting Irresistible Listings.. 37
    Optimizing Product Titles on eBay... 37
    Check Character Limit:.. 39
    Crafting Engaging Item Descriptions... 40
    Showcasing products with high quality images......................... 42

Chapter 4:... 46
Navigating eBay Tools and Features... 46
    The Power of eBay Promoted Listings.. 46
    Skyrocket Your Sales: Effective Seller Promotions on eBay.... 48

    Advanced strategies for seasoned sellers... 49

Chapter 5: **52**
Effective store management **53**
    Providing Excellent customer service on eBay................................... 57
    Building And Maintaining Positive Seller Reputation.......................... 59

Chapter 6: **59**
Understanding eBay Fees **60**
    Demystifying eBay's Fee Structure... 60
    Pricing strategies for profitability...62

Chapter 7: **64**
Strategies of Growth **65**
    Marketing your eBay store... 65
    Social media integration for Increased reach..................................... 67
    Adapting to market trends and changes... 69

Chapter 8: **71**
Common Challenges and How to Overcome Them **72**
    Avoiding Scams and Fraud.. 74
    Dealing with difficult customers... 75
    Staying compliant with eBay's policies.. 78

Frequently Asked Questions (FAQ) **85**

INTRODUCTION

Future eBay entrepreneur, Welcome to the gateway of endless possibilities! If you're holding this book "**Beginners guide to selling on eBay**", you've already taken the first step towards unlocking the vast potential that eBay holds for aspiring sellers like yourself. Allow me to extend a warm hand of congratulations and offer you a glimpse into the transformative journey that awaits you within these pages.

Selling on eBay isn't just about making a few extra bucks; it's about embracing a lifestyle of innovation, entrepreneurship, and boundless opportunity. As a beginner, stepping into the world of eBay can feel like entering a bustling marketplace where every corner holds a promise of success. Yet, amidst the excitement, questions may loom large: How do I get started? What should I sell? How do I stand out in a sea of listings?

Fear not, for within the confines of this book lies the roadmap to navigate the labyrinth of eBay selling with confidence and finesse. You see, the decision to embark on this journey isn't just about making sales; it's about seizing control of your financial destiny, unleashing your creativity, and embracing the thrill of entrepreneurship.

But why a book, you might wonder? In the age of endless online tutorials and forums, what value does a book hold for a budding eBay seller? Allow me to share a secret: amongst the chaos of information, there exists a treasure trove of wisdom and guidance tucked away within the pages of a well-crafted book. Herein lies the power of curated knowledge, distilled and refined to serve as your compass through the rough waves of eBay selling.

Within these chapters, you'll find not just answers to your burning questions, but a trusted companion to accompany you through every twist and turn of your eBay journey. Whether you're a technophile seeking to harness the power of eBay's digital landscape or a creative soul yearning to turn your passion into profit, this book holds the keys to unlock your full potential.

But let's be honest, dear reader, the allure of this book isn't merely in its promise of guidance; it's in the adventure that awaits within its pages. Picture yourself embarking on a thrilling quest, armed with knowledge as your sword and determination as your shield. Each chapter is a new frontier to explore, each lesson a stepping stone towards mastery.

So, my fellow traveler, if you've ever dreamed of turning your passion into profit, if you've ever envisioned a life of financial independence and creative fulfillment, then join me on this exhilarating journey into the heart of eBay selling. The path ahead may be challenging, but with

this book as your guide, success is not just a possibility; it's a promise waiting to be fulfilled.Are you ready to embark on your eBay selling adventure? The journey begins now !!!.

The Power of eBay: Why Sell Here?

Imagine having access to a bustling global marketplace with over 182 million active buyers, eager to discover and purchase your products. That's the magic of eBay. Selling on eBay is not just about making sales; it's about unlocking a world of opportunities with minimal upfront investment.

One of the greatest advantages of eBay is its unparalleled flexibility. You can run your business from the comfort of your home, at your own pace, and on your own schedule. No more rigid working hours or hefty rent for a physical store. eBay's user-friendly interface makes setting up your seller account and listing your products a breeze, even for beginners.

Have you ever thought about turning your unused items into cash? eBay is the perfect platform to give your old belongings a new life and make money in the process. From vintage collectibles to everyday household items, there's a buyer for almost everything on eBay.

But the benefits don't stop there. Selling on eBay allows you to tap into current trends and meet the ever-changing demands of consumers. By keeping an eye on what's hot in the marketplace, you can strategically stock products that are in high demand, ensuring your listings stand out and attract more buyers.

Trust is a cornerstone of eBay's success. With robust buyer protection policies and a transparent feedback system, buyers feel confident purchasing from reputable sellers. This trust translates into repeat business and loyal customers. As a seller, you can build a strong reputation by providing excellent customer service, ensuring your customers have a positive experience.

eBay also equips sellers with a suite of powerful tools and resources to help you succeed. From listing optimization to detailed analytics, these tools enable you to refine your selling strategies, reach a broader audience, and increase your sales. eBay's support community is also always there to offer guidance, share tips, and celebrate your milestones.

Diversifying your income has never been easier. With eBay, you can explore a wide range of product categories and find new avenues for revenue. This flexibility allows you to adapt to market trends and consumer preferences, ensuring your business remains resilient and profitable.

In essence, eBay empowers you to be your own boss. You have the freedom to set your own prices, create compelling listings, and develop unique selling strategies. The entrepreneurial opportunities are limitless, giving you the chance to build and grow your business in a dynamic and supportive environment.

So, why wait? Dive into the vibrant world of eBay, where every listing is a potential success story, and every sale brings you one step closer to your entrepreneurial dreams. Start your journey today and discover the endless possibilities that await on eBay.

How This Book Will Make You Succeed.

Embarking on your eBay selling journey can feel overwhelming, but with this book in your hands, success is not just a possibility—it's a certainty. This comprehensive guide is meticulously crafted to equip you with all the knowledge, strategies, and tools you need to thrive in the competitive world of eBay selling. Here's how this book will ensure your success:

- Step-by-Step Guidance: From setting up your eBay account to mastering advanced selling techniques, this book breaks down each step in clear, actionable terms. No matter your level of experience, you'll find detailed instructions and practical advice to guide you every step of the way.

- Insider Tips and Tricks: Benefit from the insights of seasoned eBay veterans who have navigated the platform successfully. Learn the secrets to writing compelling listings, taking high-quality photos, and optimizing your products to appear at the top of search results.
- Comprehensive Market Research: Understand what sells best on eBay and why. This book provides in-depth analysis and market trends, helping you to identify profitable niches and select products that are in high demand. You'll learn how to source items that not only sell but sell well.
- Effective Selling Strategies: Discover proven strategies to attract buyers and increase your sales. From pricing your items competitively to using eBay's promotional tools, you'll learn how to maximize your visibility and appeal to potential customers.
- Customer Service Excellence: Building a loyal customer base is crucial to your success. This book offers valuable tips on providing exceptional customer service, handling disputes professionally, and encouraging positive feedback to enhance your seller reputation.
- Financial Management: Keep your finances in check with expert advice on managing your sales revenue, tracking expenses, and understanding eBay fees. This book helps you maintain a healthy profit margin and ensures your business remains sustainable.

- Time-Saving Tools and Resources: Save time and streamline your operations with recommendations for the best eBay tools and software. Learn how to automate repetitive tasks, manage your inventory efficiently, and stay organized as your business grows.
- Real-Life Success Stories: Be inspired by real-life examples of successful eBay sellers who started just like you. Their stories and experiences provide practical insights and motivation, proving that with determination and the right guidance, you can achieve similar success.
- Troubleshooting and Problem-Solving: Face challenges head-on with a comprehensive troubleshooting section. This book addresses common issues eBay sellers encounter and provides practical solutions to keep your business running smoothly.
- Continuous Learning and Improvement: Stay ahead of the curve with tips on continuing your education and staying updated with eBay's latest features and policies. This book encourages ongoing learning to ensure your long-term success and adaptability in the ever-evolving eBay marketplace.

By the time you finish this book, you'll have a complete toolkit to conquer the eBay marketplace with confidence. You'll know exactly how to create standout listings, attract and retain customers, and grow your business sustainably. Your journey to becoming a successful eBay seller starts here, and with this book as your guide, you can rest assured that success is not just within reach—it's guaranteed.

CHAPTER 1:

Creating Your eBay Seller Account

The first step towards eBay success is creating a robust seller account. In this guide, we'll walk you through the process, from setting up your account details to understanding eBay's policies and best practices. Whether you're a casual seller or aiming for a full-fledged business, a well-crafted seller profile is the foundation for building trust and credibility with potential buyers.

Creating your eBay seller account is a straightforward process, and this step-by-step guide will walk you through each stage to ensure a smooth and successful setup.

Step one: Getting Started

Visit eBay's Homepage:

- Open your preferred web browser and go to www.ebay.com.

- Click on "Register":
- Locate the "Register" link at the top of the eBay homepage and click on it.

Step two: Account Type

- Choose "Create a Business Account" (Optional), depending on your selling goals, **you can opt for a personal or business account.**

Step three: Account Information:

- Enter Your Email Address, Provide a valid and regularly used email address.
- Create a Secure Password:
- Choose a strong password that combines letters, numbers, and symbols for security.

Step Four: Personal Information

- Enter Your Name: Provide your legal first and last name.

- Choose a User ID:Create a unique and memorable User ID. This will be your public identity on eBay.

Step Five Business Information (If Applicable)

- Enter Business Name (For Business Accounts):If you're setting up a business account, enter your business name.
- Business Contact Information:Provide business-specific contact details.

Step six:Create a PayPal Account

- Link a PayPal Account (Optional)Linking a PayPal account is recommended for smoother transactions.

Step seven:Review eBay's User Agreement and Privacy Policy

- Read and Accept Terms:Take the time to review eBay's User Agreement and Privacy Policy. Click on the checkbox to indicate that you accept these terms.

Step Eight:Confirmation Email

- Verify Your Email Address:eBay will send a confirmation email to the address you provided.

Congratulations! Your eBay Seller Account is Ready.Explore Your Seller DashboardOnce your account is confirmed, log in to your eBay account and explore your seller dashboard. Familiarize yourself with the various features and settings.

Setting Up Your Seller Profile

Creating a compelling seller profile on eBay is crucial for building trust with potential buyers and establishing credibility in the online marketplace. A well-crafted seller profile not only showcases your professionalism but also encourages buyers to choose your products over others. Follow this guide to ensure that your eBay seller profile stands out and attracts confident customers.

Step one:Access Your Seller Dashboard

- Log in to your eBay account and access your seller dashboard. Navigate to the "Account" or "Seller Hub" section, where you'll find options to manage your seller profile.

Step two:Update Personal Information

- Ensure that your personal information, such as your name and contact details, is accurate and up-to-date. This builds transparency and trust with potential buyers.

Step three:Profile Picture

- Consider adding a profile picture. While optional, a professional and friendly image of yourself can humanize your profile and create a personal connection with buyers.

Step Four: Business Information (For Business Accounts)
- If you have a business account, make sure your business name is displayed accurately. Provide relevant business contact information for smooth communication.

Step Five: User ID
- Your User ID is a key part of your identity on eBay. Ensure it is unique, easy to remember, and reflects a positive image. Avoid using personal information in your User ID for privacy reasons.

Step six: About Me Section
- Utilize the "About Me" section to share more about yourself or your business. This is an opportunity to highlight your expertise, your commitment to customer satisfaction, and any unique aspects that set you apart from other sellers.

Step seven: Feedback and Ratings

- Display your feedback score prominently. Positive feedback and high ratings provide reassurance to buyers. Address any negative feedback professionally and resolve issues promptly.

Step Eight: Customize Your Store

- If you have an eBay Store, customize it to create a branded experience for buyers. Choose a store theme, add a logo, and organize your products into categories for easy navigation.

Step nine: Payment and Return Policies

- Clearly state your accepted payment methods and return policies. Transparent policies contribute to a positive buyer experience and can increase trust in your seller profile.

step Ten: Regularly Update Your Profile:

- Keep your seller profile dynamic and relevant. Regularly update information, such as business hours, if applicable, and any changes to your contact details.

Step Eleven: Professional Communication:

- Respond promptly and professionally to buyer inquiries. Positive communication contributes to positive feedback and enhances your seller reputation.

By investing time in setting up a comprehensive and appealing seller profile, you lay the foundation for a successful eBay selling experience. A well-crafted profile not only instills confidence in buyers but also positions you as a reliable and trustworthy seller in the competitive world of online commerce.

Account Verification and Security on eBay

Ensuring the security of your eBay account is paramount for a successful and trustworthy selling experience. Account verification and robust security measures protect your personal information, financial details, and reputation as a seller. Follow this comprehensive guide to fortify the security of your eBay account.

1. Two-Step Verification:

- Enable two-step verification for an additional layer of security. This typically involves receiving a verification code on your mobile device or email when logging in.

2. Secure Password Practices

Use a strong and unique password for your eBay account. Incorporate a combination of uppercase and lowercase letters, numbers, and symbols. Avoid easily guessable information, such as birthdays or common words.

- Change your password periodically and refrain from using the same password across multiple platforms.

3. Account Verification:

- eBay may request additional verification to ensure the security of your account. This could include confirming your identity through documents or additional information.
- If prompted, follow the instructions provided by eBay to complete the verification process promptly.

4. Regularly Review Account Activity:

- Periodically review your account activity to identify any unauthorized or suspicious transactions. eBay provides a detailed account activity log that includes purchases, bids, and changes to your account settings.

5. Secure Your Email Address:

- Your email address is closely tied to your eBay account. Secure it with a strong password and enable two-step verification if your email provider supports it.
- Avoid clicking on suspicious links or downloading attachments from unknown sources in your email, as phishing attempts often target email accounts.

6. Stay Informed About Security Alerts:

- Keep an eye on security alerts and updates from eBay. Stay informed about any potential threats, scams, or security vulnerabilities that may affect your account.

7. Beware of Phishing Attempts:

- Be cautious of phishing emails or messages that appear to be from eBay. eBay will never ask you to provide sensitive information, such as passwords or credit card details, through email.
- Verify the authenticity of messages by checking your eBay messages directly through your account rather than clicking on links in emails.

8. Secure Payment Methods:

- If you link a PayPal account or other payment method to your eBay account, ensure that these accounts also have strong security measures in place. Regularly review transactions for any discrepancies.

9. Logout After Each Session:

- Always log out of your eBay account after each session, especially if using a public or shared computer. This prevents unauthorized access to your account.

10. Keep Software and Devices Updated:

- Regularly update your computer, smartphone, and any devices used for accessing eBay. Software updates often include security patches that protect against vulnerabilities.

By following these steps and remaining vigilant, you contribute to the overall security of your eBay account. A secure account not only protects your personal information but also ensures a positive and trustworthy experience for both buyers and sellers on the eBay platform.

Understanding eBay's Selling Policies and Fees

eBay's selling policies and fees are essential aspects that sellers must understand to navigate the platform effectively and ensure compliance with its rules. These policies cover various aspects of the selling process, including listing items, interacting with buyers, and fulfilling orders. eBay requires that sellers provide accurate descriptions of their items, refrain from listing prohibited or restricted items, and adhere to shipping and handling guidelines. Violations of these policies can result in penalties, such as listing removals, restrictions, or even account suspension. By adhering to eBay's policies, sellers can build a good reputation, avoid disputes, and contribute to a trustworthy marketplace.

The cost structure for selling on eBay primarily includes listing fees and final value fees. Listing fees, also known as insertion fees, are charged when a seller lists an item, with the amount varying based on factors like the category of the item and whether any optional features are selected. For instance, adding a subtitle or scheduling a listing for a specific time can incur additional charges. However, eBay often provides sellers with a number of free listings each month, which can help reduce costs. By strategically managing their listings and utilizing free listing offers, sellers can minimize their expenses and enhance their profitability.

Final value fees are incurred when an item sells and are calculated as a percentage of the total sale price, including shipping charges. These fees typically range between 10% and 15%, depending on the category of the item. Sellers need to factor these fees into their pricing strategies to ensure they maintain a healthy profit margin. Sellers who subscribe to an eBay Store can also benefit from reduced final value fees and other advantages such as increased free listings and access to promotional tools. Understanding these fees allows sellers to price their items competitively while still making a profit.

eBay also offers optional promotional tools and services designed to help sellers increase their visibility and sales. Promoted listings, for example, allow sellers to pay a fee to have their items appear higher in search results, with the fee only being charged if the item sells through the promoted listing. eBay provides sellers with various resources, including analytics, marketing tools, and customer support, to help them optimize their listings and manage their business more effectively. By taking advantage of these tools and thoroughly understanding eBay's fee structure and policies, sellers can enhance their selling experience, attract more buyers, and achieve greater success on the platform.

Choosing Between Personal and Business Accounts

Choosing between a personal and business account on eBay is a crucial decision for beginners who want to start selling on the platform. Understanding the differences and benefits of each account type can help you make an informed choice that aligns with your selling goals and needs. Both account types offer distinct features and advantages, so it's important to consider your long-term objectives and the volume of items you plan to sell.

A personal account is best suited for casual sellers or those who are looking to sell a few items occasionally. If you're cleaning out your closet, selling some used electronics, or getting rid of items you no longer need, a personal account might be the best fit. Personal accounts are straightforward to set up and offer all the basic functionalities needed to list items, communicate with buyers, and complete transactions. This account type is typically ideal for individuals who don't need plan to run a full-fledged online business.

In contrast, a business account is designed for sellers who intend to sell on a larger scale or operate a professional online store. If you plan to sell new or bulk items, or run a drop-shipping business, a business account is the way to go. Business accounts provide access to additional features such as advanced selling tools, better management options, and detailed analytics that can help you optimize your listings and increase sales. Additionally, business accounts allow you to register your account under a company name, which can enhance your brand's credibility and professionalism.

One of the main benefits of a business account is access to eBay Store subscriptions. These subscriptions offer various tiers, each with its own set of advantages such as increased free listings, reduced final value fees, and promotional tools to boost your visibility on the platform. When deciding between a personal and business account, consider your selling frequency, inventory size, and long-term goals. If you're just starting and testing the waters, a personal account can be a low-risk way to get familiar with eBay's platform and processes. As your business grows, you can upgrade to a business account to take advantage of the additional tools and resources available. However, if you already have a clear business plan and anticipate a high volume of sales, starting with a business account can save you time and provide the necessary infrastructure to support your growth from the beginning.

In conclusion, choosing the right eBay account type is a foundational step for any new seller. A personal account is suitable for occasional sellers or those new to the platform, offering simplicity and ease of use. A business account, on the other hand, caters to professional sellers with larger inventories and long-term business ambitions, providing advanced tools and support. Carefully assess your needs, selling goals, and the scale at which you intend to operate to make the best choice for your eBay journey. With the right account type, you'll be well-equipped to start selling effectively and build a successful presence on eBay.

Chapter 2:

Researching and Selecting Products

Diving into the world of eBay selling can be both exciting and rewarding, especially when you know how to research and select the right products. The key to a successful eBay business lies in understanding market trends, identifying lucrative niches, and assessing the competition. By following a detailed and strategic approach, beginners can choose products that are not only popular but also profitable, setting the stage for sustained success.

To start, it's essential to tap into market trends and understand what your buyers are looking for. One effective way to do this is by exploring eBay's "Trending on eBay" section, which showcases the latest popular items. Additionally, using tools like Google Trends can help you track the popularity of certain products over time. Look for items with steady, year-round demand rather than those that are only temporarily popular.

Next, analyzing the competition is a critical step in selecting the right products. Conduct thorough searches on eBay to see how many listings there are for the products you're considering. Examine how top sellers present their items, including their pricing strategies, listing titles, descriptions, and photos. Utilizing tools such as Terapeak, which is available through eBay, can provide valuable insights into historical sales data and competitive landscapes for specific products. This analysis will help you identify gaps in the market and opportunities to stand out from the competition with unique offerings or superior listing quality.

Once you've identified potential products and assessed the competition, it's important to evaluate the profitability of these items. Calculate all associated costs, including the purchase price, shipping fees, eBay fees, and any other expenses related to listing and selling the product. Compare these costs to the average selling price on eBay to determine your potential profit margin. Tools like eBay's fee calculator can be extremely helpful in this process. Establish relationships with reliable suppliers to secure quality products at competitive prices.

Embarking on an eBay selling journey requires careful research and thoughtful product selection. By staying attuned to market trends, analyzing competition, and ensuring profitability, beginners can make smart decisions about what to sell. This approach not only helps in selecting high-demand, low-competition products but also sets the foundation for a thriving eBay business. Investing time in thorough research will pay off by increasing your chances of success and helping you build a reputable and profitable eBay store.

Finding Your Niche: What Sells Best on eBay

Finding the right niche not only positions you to attract a dedicated customer base but also helps you stand out in a crowded marketplace. Here is a guide for identifying high-demand niches, understanding what sells best on eBay, and reassuring you that with the right approach, you can achieve success.

- The first step in finding your niche is understanding what buyers are currently looking for. Regularly explore eBay's "Trending on eBay" section, which highlights popular items and categories. Additionally, tools like Google Trends can provide insights into the popularity of specific products over time. Focus on products with consistent demand rather than fleeting trends. Seasonal items, while lucrative during peak times, should be complemented with year-round products to ensure a steady flow of sales. This approach helps mitigate risks and keeps your store active throughout the year.

- Once you have a general idea of trending products, the next step is to identify niches that balance high demand with low competition. Start by conducting searches on eBay for the products you're interested in selling. Pay close attention to the number of listings and the selling prices of these items. Tools such as Terapeak, available through eBay, can provide valuable insights into sales history, average selling prices, and the competitive landscape. Look for niches where there is steady demand but fewer sellers. This sweet spot allows you to capture a significant share of the market without facing overwhelming competition.

- Selecting a profitable niche also involves evaluating the potential profitability of your products. Calculate all associated costs, including sourcing, shipping, eBay fees, and any additional expenses. Compare these costs with the average selling prices on eBay to determine your potential profit margins. Using eBay's fee calculator can help in this process. Aim for products with healthy profit margins to ensure your business remains viable. Additionally, consider sourcing products from reliable wholesalers or manufacturers to maintain quality and consistency, which are critical for building a trustworthy brand.

- Certain categories on eBay have consistently proven to be profitable. Electronics, fashion, collectibles, home and garden items, and health and beauty products are some of the top-selling categories. However, within these broad categories, finding a specific niche can further enhance your success. For instance, in the electronics category, selling accessories like phone cases or wireless chargers might offer better margins and less competition than selling popular devices themselves. In the fashion category, vintage clothing or unique handmade accessories can attract a dedicated audience. By focusing on these specific niches, you can cater to targeted customer segments and build a loyal customer base.

- Finding your niche on eBay is a strategic process that involves understanding market trends, identifying high-demand yet low-competition areas, and ensuring product profitability. By following these steps, you position yourself to attract a dedicated customer base and achieve consistent sales. Remember, the key to eBay success lies in thorough research, careful planning, and staying adaptable to market changes. With the right approach, you can carve out a profitable niche and build a thriving eBay business.

Analyzing Market Trends and Demands

Analyzing market trends and demands is very important in identifying what products are currently popular, anticipate future demands, and strategically position your listings to attract buyers. Here is a guide to the essential steps and tools for analyzing market trends and demands to help you make informed decisions and boost your sales.

- Utilizing eBay's Built-In Tools

eBay provides several tools to help sellers analyze market trends. One of the most valuable resources is the "Trending on eBay" section, which highlights popular items and categories. This feature can give you a quick snapshot of what buyers are currently interested in. eBay's Terapeak Product Research tool also offers comprehensive insights into sales data, including average selling prices, sales volumes, and competitive analysis. By leveraging these tools, you can gather data on what products are performing well and identify emerging trends.

- Exploring External Market Research Tools

While eBay's built-in tools are incredibly useful, external market research tools can provide a broader perspective. Google Trends is a powerful tool that shows the popularity of search terms over time. By entering specific product keywords, you can see how interest has evolved and predict future trends. Another useful tool is Amazon's Best Sellers list, which can offer insights into popular items across various categories. Although the platforms differ, trends on Amazon often reflect broader market demands, providing valuable information that can inform your eBay strategy.

- Monitoring Competitor Activity

Keeping an eye on your competitors can provide valuable insights into market trends and demands. Regularly check the listings of top sellers in your niche to see what products they are offering, their pricing strategies, and how they are marketing their items. Take note of the keywords they use, the quality of their product images, and their customer engagement practices. By understanding what is working for your competitors, you can adapt your own strategies to stay competitive. Tools like Terapeak also allow you to track competitor performance, giving you a clearer picture of the competitive landscape.

- Analyzing Historical Sales Data

Historical sales data is essential for understanding market trends and forecasting future demand. Terapeak Product Research, accessible through eBay, allows you to analyze historical data for specific products over different time frames. Look for patterns such as seasonal spikes, year-over-year growth, and long-term demand stability. This information can help you plan your inventory and marketing strategies more effectively.

Below is an example of a historical sales data;

Analysis of the Graph

- **Months:** The x-axis represents the months of the year from January to December.
- **Sales Figures:** The y-axis represents the number of sales.
- **2022 Sales:** The solid blue line with circle markers represents the sales data for 2022.
- **2023 Sales:** The dashed green line with square markers represents the sales data for 2023.

- Engaging with Your Target Audience

Direct engagement with your target audience can provide firsthand insights into market demands. Use social media platforms, forums, and eBay's community boards to interact with potential buyers. Pay attention to their discussions, preferences, and feedback. Conducting surveys or polls can also be an effective way to gather information about buyer preferences and emerging trends. By staying connected with your audience, you can better understand their needs and adjust your product offerings accordingly.

- Staying Adaptable and Proactive

The e-commerce landscape is constantly evolving, and market trends can shift rapidly. To stay ahead, it's important to remain adaptable and proactive. Regularly review and update your market analysis, keeping an eye on new trends and adjusting your inventory and marketing strategies as needed. Being proactive means not only reacting to current trends but also anticipating future demands based on your analysis. This approach will help you maintain a competitive edge and ensure long-term success on eBay.

Sourcing Products:wholesales, Dropshipping and More

Sourcing products for your eBay business is a critical step that significantly impacts your success. The three primary methods of sourcing includes: wholesales, dropshipping, and other alternatives like retail arbitrage and liquidation. Understanding these options will help you make informed decisions tailored to your business needs.

Wholesaling involves purchasing products in bulk directly from manufacturers or distributors at a lower cost per unit. This method can yield higher profit margins as you benefit from reduced prices. However, it requires a significant upfront investment and storage space to manage the inventory. Reliable wholesalers can be found through directories like Alibaba and SaleHoo, and building strong relationships with them can lead to better deals and terms.

Dropshipping, on the other hand, allows you to sell products without holding any inventory. When a sale is made, the supplier ships the product directly to the customer. This model reduces startup costs and eliminates the need for storage, making it an attractive option for new sellers. However, dropshipping often results in lower profit margins and less control over product quality and shipping times. Platforms like AliExpress and Oberlo are popular for finding dropshipping suppliers.

Other sourcing methods include retail arbitrage and liquidation. Retail arbitrage involves buying discounted items from retail stores and reselling them on eBay for a profit. It requires vigilance for sales and clearance items but can yield high margins with minimal investment. Liquidation involves purchasing bulk items from businesses clearing out excess inventory or going out of business, often at a fraction of the retail price. This can be highly profitable but may result in mixed-quality products and inconsistent availability.

Each sourcing method offers unique benefits and potential drawbacks. Wholesaling provides control and higher margins but requires significant investment. Dropshipping offers low startup costs and flexibility but lower margins and less control. Alternative methods like retail arbitrage and liquidation present opportunities for high profits with minimal investment but come with their own challenges. By carefully considering these options and choosing the one that best fits your business model and resources, you can effectively source products and build a successful eBay business.

Chapter 3:

Crafting Irresistible Listings

The art of selling on eBay begins with creating compelling listings. Learn how to optimize your product titles, write engaging descriptions, and showcase your items with captivating images. We'll explore strategies for pricing your products competitively and leveraging eBay's listing features to maximize visibility and attract eager buyers

Optimizing Product Titles on eBay

Crafting compelling and optimized product titles is a critical aspect of selling on eBay. A well-optimized title not only enhances the visibility of your listings in search results but also entices potential buyers to click and explore further. Follow this comprehensive guide to master the art of optimizing your product titles on eBay.

Clarity and Relevance:

Start with a clear and concise product name that accurately describes the item you're selling. Ensure that the title is relevant to the product and matches the terms buyers are likely to search for.

Include Key Product Details:

Incorporate essential details such as brand, model, size, color, and other relevant specifications directly into the title.

Keyword Research:

Conduct thorough keyword research to identify terms that potential buyers commonly use when searching for products similar to yours. Use eBay's search bar to see suggested search terms related to your product.

Prioritize Important Information:

Place the most critical information at the beginning of the title. Buyers often skim through search results, so make sure key details are prominent.

Avoid Keyword Stuffing:

While including keywords is crucial, avoid overloading your title with excessive keywords. Maintain a balance to ensure readability and relevance.

Use Standard Spelling and Avoid Special Characters:

Use proper spelling and avoid unnecessary special characters in your titles. This ensures that your listings are easily readable and understood by both buyers and search algorithms.

Capitalization and Formatting:

Use capitalization to highlight important words in your title. Avoid writing the entire title in uppercase, as it can be perceived as spammy.

Check Character Limit:

eBay has a character limit for product titles. Be concise and make every character count. Ensure that the most critical information is within the first 80-100 characters.

Localize for Global Buyers:

If you are selling internationally, consider including regional terms and language variations to attract a broader audience.

Stay Compliant with eBay Policies:

Familiarize yourself with eBay's policies regarding product titles. Avoid misleading information, symbols, or excessive capitalization that could lead to penalties.

By implementing these strategies, you'll enhance the visibility of your listings and increase the likelihood of attracting potential buyers. Optimized product titles contribute significantly to your success on eBay by improving search rankings and ultimately driving more sales.

Crafting Engaging Item Descriptions

The item description is your canvas for painting a vivid picture of your product and persuading potential buyers to make a purchase. An engaging and informative description not only instills confidence in your buyers but also sets your listing apart in the competitive landscape of eBay. Follow this comprehensive guide to master the art of crafting compelling item descriptions that captivate your audience.

1. Start with a Clear and Concise Introduction:

Begin your item description with a concise introduction that summarizes the key features and benefits of the product.

2. Highlight Key Features:

Identify the standout features of your product and highlight them in a dedicated section. Bullet points work well for easy readability.

3. Provide Technical Specifications:

Include relevant technical details such as dimensions, materials, weight, and any other specifications that buyers might consider when making a purchase.

4. Use High-Quality Images:

Supplement your description with high-quality images that showcase the product from various angles. Add captions to your images to reinforce key points in the description.

5. Address Potential Concerns:

Anticipate and address potential concerns or questions buyers might have. This could include details about warranty, return policy, or compatibility with other products.

6. Tell a Story:

Weave a narrative around your product. Describe how it can be used or share a scenario where it would be particularly useful.

7. Use Descriptive Language:

Choose words that evoke emotions and clearly communicate the benefits of your product. Use adjectives that paint a vivid picture. e.g "plush and inviting sofa for cozy evenings."

8. Encourage Questions and Engagement:

Invite buyers to ask questions or seek clarification. This engagement not only helps buyers but also signals to eBay that your listing is active and responsive.

9. Proofread and Edit:

Ensure your description is free of spelling and grammatical errors. Proofread your content before publishing.

Showcasing products with high quality images

Creating a visually appealing product showcase with high-quality images is crucial for attracting customers and making a positive impression. Here are some tips on how to showcase products effectively using high-quality images:

1. Use Professional Photography:

- Invest in a professional photographer or learn photography techniques to capture your products in the best light.
- Ensure proper lighting, focus, and composition for each shot.

2. Highlight Key Features:

- Showcase important features and details of the product. Capture shots from different angles to provide a comprehensive view.
- Use close-ups to highlight intricate details.

3. Consistent Backgrounds:

- Maintain consistency in the background to create a cohesive look across your product images.
- Consider using a plain, neutral background that doesn't distract from the product.

4. Multiple Angles:

- Include images from various angles to give customers a complete understanding of the product's appearance.
- Display the product in use to help customers visualize its real-world application.

5. High Resolution:

- Ensure that images are of high resolution to allow customers to zoom in and examine details.
- High-resolution images convey a sense of professionalism and quality.

6. Use Props Wisely:

- Consider using props that complement the product and provide context without overshadowing it.
- Props can help customers envision how the product fits into their lives.

7. Consistent Branding:

- Maintain a consistent style and branding across all product images.
- Use a similar color palette, font, and style to reinforce your brand identity.

8. Image Editing:

- Use photo editing tools to enhance images, adjust colors, and correct any imperfections.
- Be careful not to over-edit, as authenticity is crucial.

9. Showcase Variations:

- If your product comes in different colors, sizes, or styles, showcase each variation separately.
- Provide clear labeling or categorization for easy navigation.

10. Responsive Design:

- Optimize images for various devices and screen sizes to ensure a seamless viewing experience.
- Consider implementing a responsive image gallery on your website.

11. Create a Story:

- Arrange images in a way that tells a story about the product.
- Start with an attention-grabbing image and follow with images that highlight different aspects.

12. Testimonials and Reviews:

- Integrate customer testimonials or reviews with images to build trust and credibility.
- Consider including before-and-after images if applicable.

13. Social Media Integration:

- Share your high-quality images on social media platforms to reach a wider audience.
- Use platforms like Instagram and Pinterest, known for their visual focus.

The goal is to provide potential customers with a comprehensive understanding of your product through visually appealing and high-quality images. It's an investment that can significantly impact the perception of your brand and drive sales.

Chapter 4:

Navigating eBay Tools and Features.

In the ever-evolving realm of online commerce, eBay has established itself as a global marketplace, offering a platform where sellers can connect with a vast audience. To thrive in this dynamic marketplace, understanding and effectively utilizing eBay's diverse array of tools and features is key. Whether you're a seasoned seller or just dipping your toes into online commerce, this guide is your roadmap to navigating the robust tools and features that eBay has to offer. From streamlining your listings to harnessing powerful analytics, this introduction will set the stage for your journey towards eBay mastery. Let's delve into the tools and features that will elevate your selling experience and help you carve out success in the competitive world of online retail.

The Power of eBay Promoted Listings

In the bustling marketplace of eBay, standing out is crucial for success, and eBay's Promoted Listings feature is your secret weapon for boosting visibility. This powerful tool allows sellers to enhance the discoverability of their products by strategically placing them at the forefront of search results.

How It Works:

- Select Listings: Choose the products you want to promote.
- Set Ad Rates: Determine the percentage fee you're willing to pay for each sale generated through the Promoted Listings.
- Monitor Performance: Keep a close eye on the performance analytics provided by eBay.

Benefits:

- Increased Visibility: Stand out in a crowded marketplace by ensuring your products appear prominently in search results.
- Cost-Effective Advertising: Sellers have control over advertising costs with the ability to set their own ad rates.
- Data-Driven Decisions: Leverage performance analytics to make informed decisions, refining your strategy for better results.

In the competitive world of online retail, eBay Promoted Listings give sellers a powerful edge. By strategically showcasing your products to a broader audience, you not only increase visibility but also enhance the likelihood of converting searches into successful sales.

Elevate your eBay selling experience with Promoted Listings and unlock the full potential of your online business.

Skyrocket Your Sales: Effective Seller Promotions on eBay

In the dynamic world of e-commerce, standing out from the crowd is essential for sellers looking to boost sales and attract a broader customer base. eBay provides a robust platform for sellers to create enticing promotions, offering a strategic advantage in a competitive marketplace. Let's explore how you can leverage seller promotions to supercharge your sales:

1. Types of Seller Promotions:

- Percentage Off Deals
- BOGO (Buy One, Get One) Offers
- Order Size Discounts
- Free Shipping Promotions

2. Strategic Timing:

- Flash Sales
- Holiday and Seasonal Promotions

3. Clear Communication:

- Promotional Banners
- Customized Listing Titles

4. Discount Coupons:

- Exclusive Discounts

- Time-Limited Coupons

6. Leverage eBay Tools:

- Promoted Listings
- Markdown Manager

7. Monitor and Analyze:

- Performance Metrics
- Buyer Behavior

Seller promotions on eBay are a dynamic and powerful tool for increasing sales, attracting new customers, and retaining existing ones. By strategically designing and implementing enticing promotions, sellers can create a compelling shopping experience that not only meets but exceeds buyer expectations. Stay ahead of the competition and boost your sales with well-crafted seller promotions tailored to your target audience and business goals.

Advanced strategies for seasoned sellers

As a seasoned seller on eBay, the journey to sustained success involves not just mastering the basics but also implementing advanced strategies that set you apart in a competitive e-commerce landscape. In this guide, we'll explore a range of advanced tactics that seasoned sellers can leverage to optimize their operations, maximize profits, and stay ahead of the curve.

1. Dynamic Pricing Optimization:

- *Competitive Analysis:* Regularly analyze competitor pricing and adjust your own dynamically to remain competitive while maintaining profitability.
- *Automated Tools:* Implement automated pricing tools that take into account market conditions, competitor pricing, and other variables to optimize your pricing strategy.

2. Strategic Inventory Management:

- *Demand Forecasting:* Use data analytics and historical sales data to forecast demand accurately. .
- *Seasonal Adjustments:* Adjust inventory levels strategically to align with seasonal demand fluctuations, ensuring optimal stock levels during peak periods.

3. Cross-Promotion and Upselling:

- *Bundle Offers:* Create enticing bundle offers to encourage customers to purchase complementary products together, increasing the average order value.
- *Upselling Techniques:* Implement strategic upselling by showcasing premium or upgraded items to enhance customer transactions.

4. Optimized Product Listings:

- *Keyword Optimization:* Conduct thorough keyword research and strategically incorporate high-performing keywords into product titles and descriptions for improved search visibility.
- *Enhanced Content:* Utilize eBay's enhanced content features to provide a richer and more informative shopping experience.

5. Personalized Customer Engagement:

- *Customer Segmentation:* Segment your customer base based on purchasing behavior, preferences, and demographics. Tailor marketing and communication strategies for each segment.
- *Email Marketing Automation:* Implement automated email marketing campaigns, including personalized product recommendations, exclusive offers, and targeted promotions.

6. Brand Building and Store Customization:

- *Branding:* Establish a strong brand presence by customizing your eBay store. Consistent branding fosters trust and loyalty among buyers.
- *HTML and CSS Customization:* Use HTML and CSS to customize your store layout, creating a visually appealing and unique storefront.

7. Continuous Learning and Adaptation:

- *Stay Informed:* Regularly update your knowledge on eBay policies, algorithms, and industry trends by attending webinars, conferences, and industry events.
- *Adaptability:* Maintain an adaptable mindset, experimenting with new strategies and technologies to stay ahead of evolving market dynamics.

In the dynamic world of e-commerce, seasoned sellers must continually refine and innovate their strategies to remain at the forefront. By incorporating these advanced tactics into your approach, you not only enhance your competitive edge but also position yourself for sustained success on eBay. The key lies in a commitment to continuous improvement and an ability to adapt to the ever-changing landscape of online retail.

Chapter 5:
Effective store management

In the dynamic realm of e-commerce, the success of an online store is not only determined by the quality of products but also by the effectiveness of its management.Effective store management is the linchpin of a successful e-commerce venture, encompassing a holistic approach to various business facets. From strategic inventory management and personalized customer engagement to optimized product listings and efficient order fulfillment, it involves meticulous planning and execution. Marketing strategies, data-driven decision-making, and the integration of technology play pivotal roles, fostering visibility and enhancing the overall shopping experience. Financial oversight, adaptability to market trends, and a commitment to continuous improvement complete the picture. By embracing these principles, businesses can navigate the complexities of online retail, fostering growth, customer satisfaction, and long-term success.

Organizing Your Inventory for Business Success

Effectively organizing your inventory is a cornerstone of efficient business operations, ensuring that products are readily accessible, order fulfillment is streamlined, and customer satisfaction is optimized. Here's a guide to mastering the art of inventory organization:

1. Categorization and Segmentation:

- *Group Similar Items:* Categorize products based on similarities in type, size, or usage to streamline storage and retrieval processes.
- *ABC Analysis:* Prioritize items based on sales frequency to allocate storage space accordingly—high-selling items in easily accessible areas.

2. Strategic Storage Systems:

- *Utilize Shelving and Racking:* Invest in shelving and racking systems to maximize vertical space, ensuring an organized and easily navigable storage environment.
- *Bin and Drawer Systems:* Employ bins, drawers, or labeled containers for smaller items, minimizing the risk of misplacement.

3. Clear Identification and Labeling:

- *Barcoding and RFID:* Implement barcode or RFID systems for accurate tracking and swift identification of items during inventory checks.
- *Clearly Labeled Shelves:* Ensure shelves and storage bins are clearly labeled, facilitating quick and error-free picking.

4. First-In-First-Out (FIFO) System:

- *Rotation Strategy:* Adopt the FIFO system to minimize product spoilage or obsolescence by using older stock first.
- *Expiry Date Tracking:* Clearly mark and monitor products with expiration dates, if applicable, to avoid selling expired goods.

5. Regular Audits and Cycle Counts:

- *Scheduled Audits:* Conduct regular inventory audits to reconcile physical stock with recorded levels and identify discrepancies promptly.
- *Cycle Counts:* Implement cycle counting, focusing on specific product categories at different intervals, reducing disruptions in daily operations.

6. Supplier Collaboration:

- *Communication Channels:* Maintain open lines of communication with suppliers to streamline restocking processes, negotiate favorable terms, and stay informed about product availability.

- *Vendor-Managed Inventory (VMI):* Explore VMI agreements with key suppliers, allowing them to manage your inventory levels based on pre-established criteria.

7.. Employee Training and Accountability:

- *Training Programs:* Provide comprehensive training for staff on inventory management procedures, emphasizing accuracy and efficiency.
- *Accountability Measures:* Implement accountability measures to ensure that employees adhere to established protocols, minimizing errors and discrepancies.

8. Adaptability and Continuous Improvement:

- *Feedback Mechanisms:* Solicit feedback from employees involved in inventory management to identify bottlenecks and areas for improvement.
- *Adapt to Changing Needs:* Stay adaptable to changes in product lines, market demands, and business growth, adjusting inventory management strategies accordingly.

By implementing these organizational strategies, businesses can maintain a well-ordered inventory, ensuring smoother operations, reducing costs, and ultimately enhancing customer satisfaction through timely and accurate order fulfillment.

Providing Excellent customer service on eBay

Providing excellent customer service on eBay is crucial for building trust, attracting repeat business, and maintaining a positive seller reputation. Here are some tips to ensure you deliver exceptional customer service on the eBay platform:

1. **Clear and Accurate Item Descriptions:**

   - Provide detailed and accurate descriptions of your items. Include information about the product's features, condition, and any relevant specifications.

2. **High-Quality Images:**

   - Include clear, high-resolution images of your products from various angles. This helps buyers get a better understanding of the item's condition and appearance.

3. **Prompt Communication:**

   - Respond to buyer inquiries and messages promptly. Address any questions or concerns they may have and provide helpful, friendly, and professional responses.

4. **Fast Shipping:**

   - Ship items promptly after receiving payment. Fast and reliable shipping enhances the overall customer experience.

5. Secure Packaging:
- Pack items securely to prevent damage during transit. Proper packaging not only protects the item but also demonstrates your commitment to delivering quality products to your customers.

6. Offer Special Deals and Promotions:
- Consider offering special deals or promotions, such as discounted shipping on multiple items or limited-time sales.

7. Regularly Update Your eBay Store:
- Keep your eBay store updated with new products, promotions, and relevant information. An active and well-maintained store can attract more customers and showcase your commitment to your eBay business.

8. Educate Buyers:
- Provide information and guides related to your products. Educated buyers are often more satisfied, and it reduces the likelihood of misunderstandings or dissatisfaction.

By consistently providing excellent customer service on eBay, you not only enhance the buying experience for your customers but also contribute to the long-term success and growth of your online business.

Building And Maintaining Positive Seller Reputation

Building and maintaining a positive seller reputation online is essential. Provide accurate product descriptions, high-quality images, and competitive pricing for transparency. Prioritize prompt communication, fast shipping, and secure packaging to showcase professionalism. Encourage positive reviews from satisfied customers to build credibility. Maintain consistency in product quality, customer service, and shipping practices. Handle customer issues promptly and professionally to turn challenges into positive experiences. Clearly outline return and refund policies to manage customer expectations.

Stay informed about platform policies and adapt practices accordingly. Regularly update product listings and remove unavailable items to prevent negative experiences. Proactively address customer concerns and seek ways to improve products and services based on feedback. Embrace a customer-centric approach to foster trust and credibility.

Chapter 6:
Understanding eBay Fees

Understanding eBay fees is crucial for sellers to effectively manage their costs and maximize profitability. eBay charges sellers various fees, including an insertion fee for listing an item, final value fees based on the item's sale price, and additional fees for optional listing upgrades. Sellers should be aware of the fee structure, which can vary based on the type of item, format, and seller level. Consider factors like shipping costs and payment method fees, as they also impact overall expenses. Regularly review eBay's fee policies and use the fee calculator to estimate costs accurately. By understanding and carefully managing fees, sellers can optimize their pricing strategies and enhance their overall eBay selling experience.

Demystifying eBay's Fee Structure

Demystifying eBay's fee structure is critical for sellers to effectively manage their expenses and maximize profits. eBay employs a comprehensive fee system that includes various charges, and understanding these intricacies is key to navigating the platform successfully. Here's a breakdown of eBay's fee structure:

1. **Insertion Fees:**
   - eBay charges an insertion fee for listing an item. This fee is based on the type of listing (auction-style or fixed price), the category of the item, and any optional listing upgrades.
2. **Final Value Fees (FVF):**
   - The final value fee is a percentage of the total amount a buyer pays for an item, including shipping and handling.
3. **Optional Listing Upgrades:**
   - Sellers can choose optional upgrades for their listings, such as adding subtitles, extra photos, or highlighting the listing. Each of these upgrades incurs an additional fee, and sellers need to weigh the benefits against the costs.
4. **Promoted Listings:**
   - Sellers can opt for promoted listings to increase the visibility of their products.
5. **Shipping Costs and Impact on Fees:**
   - Shipping costs are a crucial component of eBay fees. Final value fees are assessed on the total amount the buyer pays, including shipping. Sellers need to factor this into their pricing strategy to ensure they cover expenses and maintain profitability.
6. **Payment Processing Fees:**

- eBay manages payments for many sellers, and payment processing fees are applied to the transaction amount, including the item price, shipping, and any sales tax.

7. Fee Calculators:

- eBay provides fee calculators that allow sellers to estimate their fees based on various scenarios. These tools are valuable for planning and setting competitive prices.

8. Stay Informed about Policy Changes:

- eBay occasionally updates its fee structure and policies. Sellers should stay informed about any changes through official communications and updates from eBay.

Pricing strategies for profitability.

Demystifying eBay's fee structure empowers sellers to make informed decisions about their pricing, listing strategies, and overall financial management. Regularly reviewing and optimizing these strategies ensures that sellers can navigate the platform successfully and maximize their profitability.

Implementing effective pricing strategies is crucial for maximizing profitability in business. Here are key considerations and strategies to optimize pricing for increased profitability:

1. Cost-Plus Pricing:

- Determine the total cost of producing or acquiring a product, then add a markup to establish the selling price.

2. Competitive Pricing:

- Analyze competitors' pricing for similar products and position your prices competitively.

3. Value-Based Pricing:

- Set prices based on the perceived value of your product or service in the eyes of customers.

4. Dynamic Pricing:

- Adjust prices in real-time based on market demand, seasonality, or other relevant factors. This strategy allows for flexibility and responsiveness to changing market conditions.

5. Subscription and Tiered Pricing:

- Introduce subscription models or tiered pricing structures to encourage customer loyalty and provide options for different customer segments with varying needs and budgets.

6. Geographic Pricing:

- Consider adjusting prices based on geographic locations, accounting for regional differences in purchasing power and market conditions..

7. Limited-Time Offers:
- Introduce scarcity by offering limited-time promotions or exclusive deals. This can create a sense of urgency and drive quicker purchasing decisions.

8. Relationship-Based Pricing:

- Offer special pricing or loyalty programs for repeat customers. Building long-term relationships can lead to a more stable and profitable customer base.

9. Collaborative Pricing with Suppliers:

- Negotiate favorable terms with suppliers to lower input costs, contributing to higher profit margins without necessarily increasing prices for customers.

Effective pricing strategies involve a combination of these approaches, tailored to the specific business, industry, and target audience. Regularly evaluate and adapt pricing strategies to ensure ongoing profitability and competitiveness.

Chapter 7:

Strategies of Growth

eBay focuses on growth through global expansion, technological innovation, and strategic partnerships. Diversification of product offerings and a strong mobile presence contribute to an enhanced marketplace. Seller empowerment, AI-driven personalization, and buyer loyalty programs drive increased engagement. Streamlined checkout processes and sustainability initiatives further boost customer satisfaction and appeal. These combined strategies position eBay as a competitive and evolving platform in the dynamic e-commerce landscape.

Marketing your eBay store

Effectively marketing your eBay store is crucial for increasing visibility, attracting customers, and driving sales. Here are key strategies for promoting your eBay store:

1. **Optimized eBay Listings:**
   - Craft compelling, keyword-rich titles and detailed product descriptions to improve search visibility within eBay. Utilize high-quality images to showcase your products.

2. **eBay Store Subscription:**
   - Consider subscribing to an eBay store, which provides additional marketing tools, customization options, and discounted fees.

3. **Cross-Promotion:**
   - Cross-promote related items within your store to encourage customers to explore additional products, increasing the likelihood of multiple purchases.

4. **Social Media Marketing:**
   - Share your eBay store and product listings on social media platforms. Utilize Facebook, Instagram, Twitter, and other channels to reach a broader audience.

5. **Email Marketing:**

- Build and maintain an email list of customers who have opted in to receive updates.

6. Paid Advertising:
- Utilize eBay's sponsored listings feature for paid advertising. This can increase the visibility of your products in search results and attract more potential customers.

7. Optimize for Mobile Users:
- Ensure that your eBay store is mobile-friendly, as a significant portion of users accesses the platform through smartphones. A responsive design enhances the user experience.

8. **Implement SEO Best Practices**:
- Apply search engine optimization (SEO) best practices within your eBay store, using relevant keywords in titles, descriptions, and other fields to improve discoverability.

9. Run Limited-Time Promotions:
- Create a sense of urgency by running limited-time promotions or flash sales. This can encourage quicker decision-making among potential buyers.

By implementing a combination of these strategies, you can effectively market your eBay store, increase visibility, and attract a broader audience of potential customers. Regularly evaluate the performance of your marketing efforts and adjust strategies based on customer behavior and market trends.

Social media integration for Increased reach

Integrating social media into your marketing strategy is a powerful way to increase the reach of your eBay store and connect with a wider audience. Here are key strategies for effective social media integration:

1. **Choose Relevant Platforms:**
   - Identify the social media platforms that align with your target audience and product niche. Common platforms include Facebook, Instagram, Twitter, Pinterest, and LinkedIn.
2. **Create a Consistent Brand Presence:**
   - Maintain a cohesive brand presence across your eBay store and social media profiles. Use consistent branding elements, such as logos, colors, and messaging, to enhance brand recognition.
3. **Share Compelling Content:**
   - Regularly share engaging content, including product images, promotions, and behind-the-scenes glimpses. Diversify content to include videos, customer testimonials, and relevant industry news.
4. **Engage with Your Audience:**
   - Actively engage with your social media audience by responding to comments, messages, and mentions.
5. **Host Contests and Giveaways:**
   - Organize contests or giveaways on social media platforms to encourage user participation, increase brand visibility, and attract new followers.

6. Share User-Generated Content:

- Encourage customers to share their experiences with your products and repost user-generated content. This builds authenticity and trust while expanding your content reach.

6. Promote Limited-Time Offers:

- Create a sense of urgency by promoting limited-time offers or exclusive deals on social media. This can drive traffic to your eBay store and boost sales.

7. Optimize Posting Times:

- Analyze the peak engagement times for your audience on different social media platforms and schedule posts accordingly.

8. Use Social Media Analytics:

- Utilize analytics tools provided by social media platforms to track the performance of your posts, understand audience behavior, and refine your strategy for maximum impact.

By integrating these strategies, you can effectively leverage social media to increase the reach of your eBay store, engage with potential customers, and drive sales. Regularly assess the performance of your social media efforts and adjust your approach based on evolving trends and audience preferences.

Adapting to market trends and changes

Adapting to market trends and changes is essential for businesses to remain relevant and thrive in a dynamic environment. Here are key strategies for successfully navigating shifts in market dynamics:

1.**Continuous Monitoring:**

Regularly monitor industry trends, consumer behavior, and competitive landscapes to stay informed about changes affecting your market.

2 .**Flexibility and Agility:**

Cultivate a culture of flexibility within your organization. Be prepared to pivot strategies quickly in response to emerging trends or unexpected market shifts.

3.**Customer Feedback and Data Analysis:**

Actively seek customer feedback and utilize data analytics to understand customer preferences.

4.**Innovation and R&D:**

Invest in research and development to foster innovation. Stay ahead of the curve by introducing new products or services that align with evolving market demands.

5. Adaptive Marketing Strategies:

Adjust marketing strategies in response to changing consumer behaviors and preferences.

6. Employee Training and Development:

Ensure that your workforce is equipped with the skills needed to adapt to technological advancements and changing market dynamics. Continuous training fosters adaptability.

7. Risk Management:

Develop robust risk management strategies to identify and mitigate potential challenges arising from market fluctuations, economic shifts, or unforeseen circumstances.

8. Scenario Planning:

Conduct scenario planning exercises to anticipate potential market shifts and develop strategies to address various future scenarios.

9. Regular Business Assessments:

Conduct regular assessments of your business performance and strategies. This allows for timely adjustments to align with market changes and emerging opportunities.

By adopting a proactive and adaptive mindset, businesses can position themselves to thrive in an ever-changing marketplace. The ability to recognize and respond to market trends ensures resilience and long-term success.

Chapter 8:

Common Challenges and How to Overcome Them

Selling on eBay can be a lucrative venture, but like any business, it comes with its own set of challenges. Understanding eBay's complex policies and fee structures can be daunting for beginners. Misunderstanding these can lead to unexpected costs and potential account suspension. To overcome this, it is essential to thoroughly research eBay's Seller Center resources to grasp their rules and regulations. Utilizing eBay's fee calculator helps in estimating selling costs, including listing fees, final value fees, and PayPal fees.

- Creating effective listings that attract buyers and stand out among millions of others is another significant challenge. High-quality photos are crucial, so investing in a good camera or smartphone to take clear, high-resolution photos from multiple angles is beneficial. Detailed descriptions that include item specifics, condition, and any flaws help build trust with potential buyers. Optimizing listings with relevant keywords improves visibility in search results, and researching similar items to price products competitively can make a big difference. Utilizing eBay's "Best Offer" feature can also attract more buyers by offering them flexibility.

- Managing inventory to prevent overselling can be challenging, especially as your business grows. Utilizing inventory management software like eBay's Selling Manager or third-party tools can help track stock levels accurately. Conducting regular inventory audits ensures that listings are accurate, and setting up automated reordering for high-demand items can prevent stockouts, keeping your business running smoothly.
- Customer service and handling returns can be time-consuming and stressful. Clearly stating return and refund policies on listings sets customer expectations. Responding to inquiries promptly and professionally through eBay's messaging system helps maintain organized and efficient communication. Aiming for high levels of customer satisfaction to receive positive feedback and maintain a good seller rating is crucial for building a trustworthy reputation.
- Ensuring timely and cost-effective shipping is vital for customer satisfaction. Offering multiple shipping options caters to different buyer preferences and urgency. Using eBay's shipping calculator helps determine accurate shipping costs to avoid undercharging. Providing tracking information enhances transparency and trust, while investing in quality packaging materials and following best practices protect items during transit.

- Standing out in a crowded marketplace with numerous competitors can be tough. Identifying and emphasizing your unique selling proposition (USP) can help differentiate your products. Focusing on a niche market with less competition allows you to establish yourself as an expert. Utilizing eBay's promotional tools, such as Promoted Listings, increases visibility, and leveraging social media and email marketing drives traffic to your listings.
- Building a positive reputation and gaining trust from buyers takes time. Consistently offering high-quality products and services is key. Encouraging satisfied customers to leave positive feedback enhances your credibility. Handling disputes and returns professionally and swiftly helps maintain a good seller rating, which is crucial for long-term success.
- The e-commerce market is dynamic, and trends can change rapidly. Regular market research keeps you informed about industry trends and buyer preferences. Being flexible and willing to adapt your product offerings and business strategies to meet changing market demands is essential. Continuously educating yourself through eBay webinars, forums, and other resources keeps you ahead of the curve and better equipped to handle market shifts.

Avoiding Scams and Fraud

Avoiding scams and fraud is essential for a successful and secure selling experience on eBay. One effective strategy is to thoroughly vet buyers before completing transactions. Start by checking the buyer's feedback score and reading reviews from other sellers. Buyers with high feedback scores and positive reviews are generally more reliable. Be cautious with buyers who have recently created their accounts or have numerous negative feedback comments. Utilize eBay's buyer requirements settings to block buyers with unpaid item strikes or a history of policy violations, further safeguarding your sales.

Using secure payment methods is another crucial step to prevent fraud. eBay recommends using PayPal or other eBay-approved payment methods because they offer protection for both buyers and sellers. Avoid accepting payments outside of these channels, as this can leave you vulnerable to scams. Conduct all communications and transactions through eBay's platform to maintain a record of interactions, which can be essential evidence in case of disputes. Additionally, never share personal information, such as your bank details or address, with buyers. eBay's messaging system is designed to protect your privacy and security, so it is important to use it for all buyer communications.

Finally, protecting yourself involves documenting all aspects of the sale. Take detailed photographs of the item before shipping and keep copies of all correspondence. When shipping items, use a tracked and insured shipping service and provide the buyer with a tracking number. This reassures the buyer and provides proof of shipment in case of disputes. If a buyer claims an item was not received, you will have evidence to support your case. By following these precautions and staying informed about common scam tactics, you can sell on eBay with confidence and peace of mind. Adhering to these best practices ensures a secure and successful selling experience.

Dealing with difficult customers.

Dealing with difficult customers is a challenge that every seller will face at some point, and handling these situations effectively is important for maintaining a successful eBay business. Here are some strategies to help you manage difficult customers and turn potentially negative experiences into positive outcomes.

Maintain Professionalism and Composure

When dealing with a difficult customer, it's essential to stay calm and professional. Reacting emotionally or defensively can escalate the situation and damage your reputation. Instead, respond with a polite and respectful tone, even if the customer is upset or unreasonable. Acknowledge their concerns and show empathy by expressing that you understand their frustration. This can help to de-escalate the situation and create a more constructive dialogue.

Respond Promptly and Clearly

Timely communication is key to managing customer complaints effectively. Respond to customer inquiries and complaints as soon as possible, ideally within 24 hours. This shows that you value their business and are committed to resolving their issue. When responding, be clear and concise. Provide detailed answers to their questions and explain the steps you will take to address their concerns. Clear communication can prevent misunderstandings and demonstrate your professionalism.

Offer Solutions and Alternatives

When a customer is unhappy, offering practical solutions can help to resolve the issue quickly. If the customer received a damaged or incorrect item, apologize and offer to send a replacement or issue a refund. If the item is delayed, provide tracking information and an estimated delivery date. In cases where the customer is dissatisfied with the product, consider offering a partial refund or a discount on future purchases as a goodwill gesture. Providing solutions shows that you are willing to go the extra mile to ensure customer satisfaction.

Utilize eBay's Resolution Center

For disputes that cannot be resolved through direct communication, eBay's Resolution Center is a valuable resource. Encourage the customer to open a case through the Resolution Center, where eBay can mediate the situation. This formal process ensures that both parties have a fair opportunity to present their case and reach a resolution. eBay's Resolution Center can handle issues such as items not received, items not as described, and return requests, providing an impartial platform to resolve conflicts.

Learn from Feedback and Reviews

Negative feedback and reviews, while unpleasant, can offer valuable insights into areas where you can improve. Analyze the feedback to identify recurring issues or common complaints. Use this information to make necessary adjustments to your business practices, whether it's improving product descriptions, enhancing packaging, or refining your communication strategy. Proactively addressing these areas can help to prevent future problems and improve overall customer satisfaction.

Staying compliant with eBay's policies.

The first step in staying compliant with eBay's policies is ensuring compliance is thoroughly understanding eBay's Seller Center resources. These resources provide comprehensive information about eBay's rules and regulations, including listing policies, prohibited items, and intellectual property rights. Regularly reviewing these policies helps sellers stay updated on any changes or new requirements. Additionally, familiarizing yourself with eBay's User Agreement and Privacy Policy ensures that you are aware of your obligations and the standards you need to meet as an eBay seller.

To maintain compliance, it's crucial to follow best practices in listing and selling your items. Accurate and honest descriptions are paramount; misrepresenting an item's condition or features can lead to disputes and negative feedback, and it may even result in account suspension. High-quality photos that clearly show the item from multiple angles can prevent misunderstandings about the product's condition.

Furthermore, adhering to eBay's guidelines for item categories and keywords ensures that your listings are not flagged for violations. Avoiding the sale of prohibited items and adhering to any category-specific policies is also critical. For example, there are strict regulations for selling items like electronics, collectibles, and health-related products, which must be meticulously followed to avoid penalties.

Lastly, effective communication with buyers plays a significant role in staying compliant. Promptly responding to inquiries and resolving issues amicably demonstrates your commitment to customer service and can prevent disputes from escalating to eBay's Resolution Center. Maintaining transparency in your return and refund policies helps manage buyer expectations and reduces the likelihood of negative feedback or complaints. By consistently monitoring your account for policy adherence and addressing any warnings or notifications from eBay promptly, you can safeguard your seller account. Regularly engaging with eBay's seller community forums and participating in webinars can also provide valuable insights and updates, helping you stay compliant and successful in the competitive eBay marketplace.

Frequently Asked Questions (FAQ)

1. **How do I create an eBay account?**
   - To create an eBay account, visit the eBay website and click on the "Register" or "Sign Up" option. Follow the prompts to provide necessary information such as your email address, name, and password.

2. **What items are not allowed to be sold on eBay?**

   - eBay prohibits the sale of certain items, including illegal items, prescription drugs, firearms, and certain types of adult content. Refer to eBay's prohibited and restricted items policy for a comprehensive list.

3. **How can I list an item for sale on eBay?**

    ○ To list an item, log in to your eBay account, click on "Sell" at the top of the page, and follow the step-by-step process to create a listing. Provide accurate details about your item, set a price, and choose your preferred shipping options.

4. **What are eBay fees and how are they calculated?**

    ○ eBay charges fees for listing items and a final value fee based on the sale price. The exact fees depend on factors like the type of listing, category, and any optional upgrades. eBay provides a fee calculator for sellers to estimate costs.

5. **How does eBay's bidding system work?**

    ○ eBay uses a bidding system for auction-style listings. Buyers place bids on items, and the highest bidder at the end of the auction wins. Alternatively, sellers can choose to list items with a fixed price (Buy It Now) without bidding.

6. **Can I cancel a bid on eBay?**

- In general, bids on eBay are considered binding contracts, and canceling a bid is discouraged. However, there are specific situations, such as a bidder making a mistake, where eBay allows bid retractions. Sellers can also cancel bids under certain circumstances.

7. **How can I protect myself from scams on eBay?**

- To protect yourself, use secure payment methods, be cautious of suspicious emails or messages, and carefully review a seller's feedback and ratings. eBay's Buyer Protection program offers additional safeguards for eligible purchases.

8. **What is the eBay Global Shipping Program?**

- The Global Shipping Program allows sellers to ship items internationally while eBay handles customs and import duties. Buyers from eligible countries can purchase items with international shipping through this program.

9. **How can I improve my seller rating on eBay?**

- To improve your seller rating, provide accurate item descriptions, ship items promptly, communicate effectively with buyers, and resolve any issues professionally. Positive feedback from satisfied customers contributes to a higher rating.

10. **Can I change or upgrade my eBay store subscription?**

    - Yes, sellers can change or upgrade their eBay store subscription at any time. Navigate to the "Subscription" section in the Seller Hub to make adjustments based on your business needs.

Remember to refer to eBay's official help and support resources for the most accurate and up-to-date information regarding frequently asked questions

www.ingramcontent.com/pod-product-compliance
Lightning Source LLC
Chambersburg PA
CBHW082238220526
45479CB00005B/1269